How to Build
BOX CARS
AND
TRUCKS

Jeff Barger

Rourke
Educational Media

rourkeeducationalmedia.com

Teaching Focus:

Consonant Blends- Look in the book to find words that begin with a consonant blend such as *dr* or *gl*.

Before Reading:

Building Academic Vocabulary and Background Knowledge

Before reading a book, it is important to set the stage for your child or student by using pre-reading strategies. This will help them develop their vocabulary, increase their reading comprehension, and make connections across the curriculum.

1. Read the title and look at the cover. *Let's make predictions about what this book will be about.*
2. Take a picture walk by talking about the pictures/photographs in the book. Implant the vocabulary as you take the picture walk. Be sure to talk about the text features such as headings, Table of Contents, glossary, bolded words, captions, charts/diagrams, or Index.
3. Have students read the first page of text with you then have students read the remaining text.
4. Strategy Talk – use to assist students while reading.
   - Get your mouth ready
   - Look at the picture
   - Think…does it make sense
   - Think…does it look right
   - Think…does it sound right
   - Chunk it – by looking for a part you know
5. Read it again.
6. After reading the book complete the activities below.

Content Area Vocabulary

body
edge
length
opposite
pierce
width

After Reading:

Comprehension and Extension Activity

After reading the book, work on the following questions with your child or students in order to check their level of reading comprehension and content mastery.

1. *Describe how to make a cereal box car or truck.* (Summarize)
2. *The wheels of the car are connected by what piece?* (Asking questions)
3. *What object could be used to make the cab of your truck?* (Asking questions)
4. *How is the cereal box car or truck like cars and trucks you see on the road?* (Text to self connection)

Extension Activity

Ask some friends to have a series of contests where you race your cereal box cars or trucks. Create a chart where you record how far your vehicles traveled each contest. Use a yardstick or meter stick to measure the distance.

Table of Contents

Roll With It!

Let's go racing! In the house? Yes! We will make cereal box cars and trucks.

Make sure you have an adult's permission or supervision to use the tools and materials.

You will need:

cereal box

four CDs

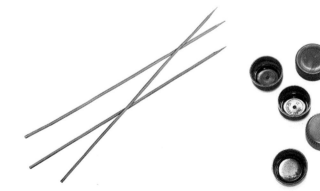

hot glue gun   3 wooden
skewers

8 bottle caps

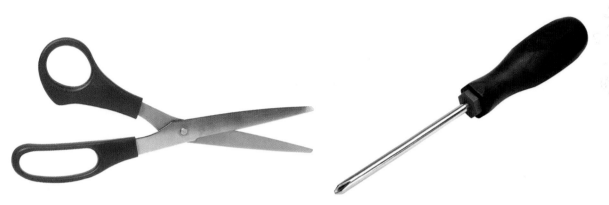

scissors

Phillips-head screwdriver

2 drinking straws

rubber bands

paper clip

Ready? Set? Cut!

Open the box. Remove the bag.

Find a container to store the unused cereal.

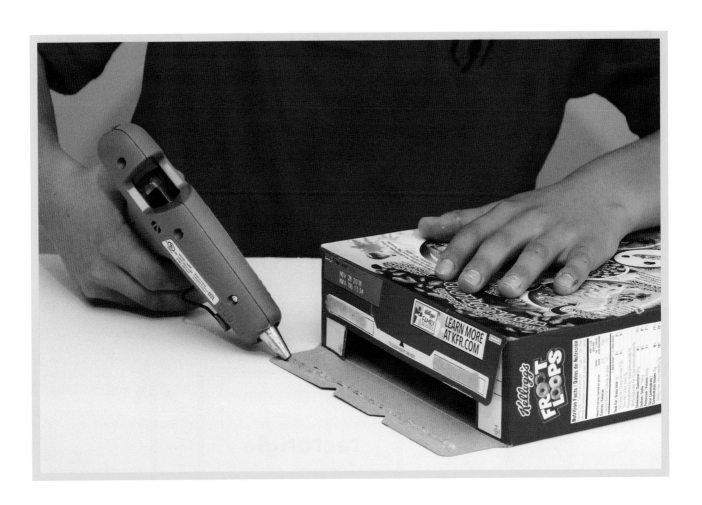

Glue the box shut. The box is the **body** of the car.

Find the bottom **edge** of the box. Cut a rectangle in the middle. The rectangle **length** is three inches (7.62 centimeters). The **width** is two inches (5.08 centimeters). Cut a similar rectangle in the front of the box at the top.

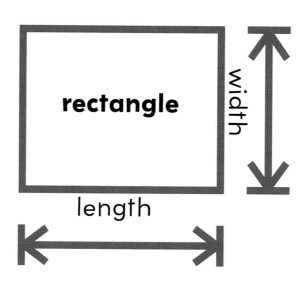

rectangle

width

length

Measure the box to find the middle.

11

The Wheels on the Box

Cut a drinking straw in half. Glue one half to the bottom left of the box. Glue the other half to the bottom right side.

Measure the straw to find the halfway point.

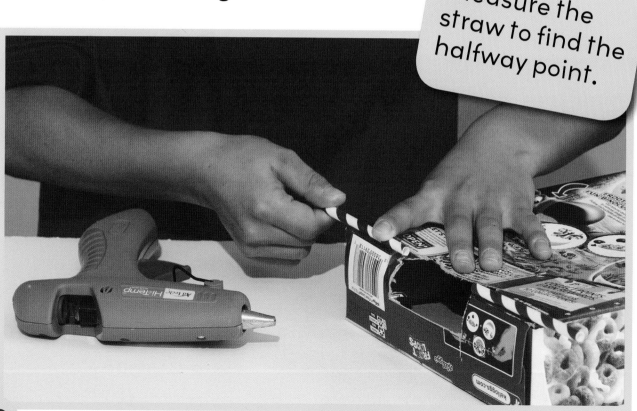

An axle allows wheels to move.

Cut the other straw in half. Place a skewer in the straws for the axle.

Glue two straw pieces on the **opposite** bottom end of the box. Place a skewer in the straws.

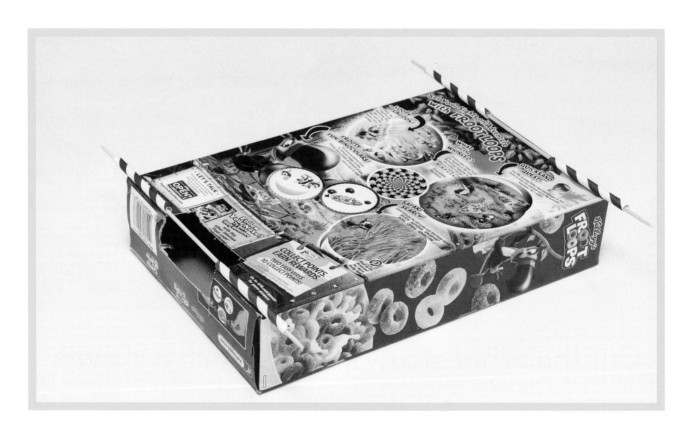

Do you want to make a truck? Place a tissue box on top of the cereal box to make the cab. Cut the top of the back half of the cereal box to make a truck bed.

Use the screwdriver to **pierce** a hole in the center of each cap. Glue a cap to the center of each side of the CDs. Place a CD on each end of a skewer. Now you have four wheels!

Power Up!

Cut a skewer in half. Glue it across the hole in the front of the box.

Next, make a chain of rubber bands.

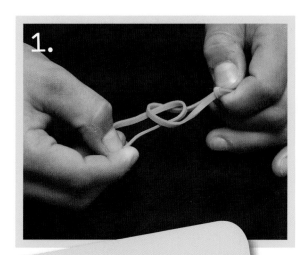

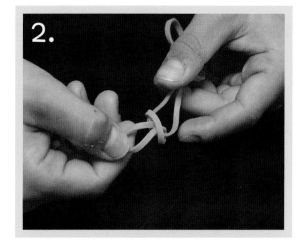

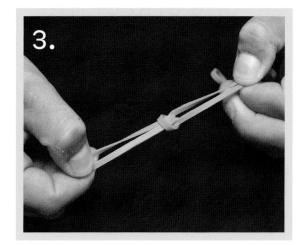

1. Overlap two rubber bands.
2. Take the left end of the right rubber band and pull it under the right end of the left rubber band.
3. Pull tight.

Glue a paper clip on the middle of the back skewer. That will be a hook for the chain.

Loop one end of the rubber-band chain to the front axle. Hook the other end to the paper clip.

Find a clear space about 20 feet (6 meters) long to race your car.

Turn the back wheels to wind up the car.

Let go and watch it run!

Photo Glossary

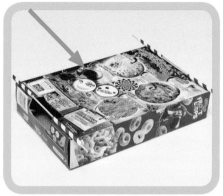

body (BAH-dee): The main or central part of something.

edge (EJ): The part of an object or area that is farthest from the center.

length (LENGKTH): The measurement of something from end to end.

opposite (AH-puh-zit): Across from or facing.

pierce (PEERS): To make a hole in something.

width (WIDTH): The distance from one side of something to the other.

Index

Further Reading

Dees, Sarah, *Awesome Lego Creations*, Page Street Publishing, 2016.

Lacey, Saskia and Sodomka, Martin, *How to Build a Car: A high-speed adventure of mechanics, teamwork, and friendship (Technical Tales)*, Walter Foster Jr, 2015.

Priddy, Roger, *First 100 Trucks*, Priddy Bicknell Books, 2016.

Meet The Author!
www.meetREMauthors.com

About the Author

Jeff Barger is a literacy specialist who lives in North Carolina. He would like a rubber-band-powered car that he could drive to work.

PHOTO CREDITS: All photography by Blue Door Education except pages 6-7: cereal box © MAHATHIR MOHD YASIN, CDs © NDT, glue gun © Coprid, skewers © modustollens, scissors © Hurst Photo, screwdriver © vincent noel, drinking straws © ang intaravichian, rubber bands © Cherkas; page 10 diagram © GzP_Design; page 23 olives © Anna Kucherova—all from Shutterstock.com

Edited by: Keli Sipperley

Produced by Blue Door Education for Rourke Educational Media.
Cover and page design: by Nicola Stratford
www.nicolastratford.com

Library of Congress PCN Data

How to Build Box Cars and Trucks / Jeff Barger
(Step-By-Step Projects)
ISBN 978-1-64156-431-1 (hard cover)
ISBN 978-1-64156-557-8 (soft cover)
ISBN 978-1-64156-678-0 (e-Book)
Library of Congress Control Number: 2018930453

Rourke Educational Media
Printed in the United States of America, North Mankato, Minnesota